EXITS

Selected Poems

Stephen C. Pollock

Windtree
Press

Published by Windtree Press | windtreepress.com
Book design by Stephen C. Pollock.
Technical support provided by Durgapu Kamalakar.
"Betterflies" reproduced with permission of Julia Lillard.
Fire Pit Art image reproduced with permission of Heather Graviss Photography.
Printed in the United States of America.

Publisher's Cataloging-in-Publication Data
Names: Pollock, Stephen C., author.
Title: Exits : selected poems / Stephen C. Pollock.
Description: Includes index. | Corvallis, OR: Windtree Press, 2023.
Identifiers: LCCN: 2023901120
ISBN: 978-1-957638-68-3 (print) | 978-1-957638-67-6 (ebook) | 978-1-957638-69-0 (audio)
Subjects: LCSH Poetry, American. | American poetry--21st century. | Mortality--Poetry. | Nature--Poetry. | Death--Poetry. | BISAC POETRY / General | POETRY / Subjects & Themes / Animals & Nature | POETRY / Subjects & Themes / Death, Grief, Loss
Classification: LCC PS3616.055 E95 2023 | DDC 811.6--dc23

Preface

Every life is finite. Though circumstance and timing may vary, death remains the one inescapable attribute of the human condition. Awareness of this inevitability and recognition of the transient nature of our biological selves profoundly affect each person's perspective on their life and its meaning.

The poems in this book relate to one or more aspects of mortality—disease and decline, death and remembrance. Many of the images and metaphors are drawn from nature. In addition, each poem is paired with a piece of artwork intended to resonate with the writing and enhance the reader's experience.

In a world ravaged by contagion, famine and war, *Exits* dovetails with the prevailing zeitgeist.

Contents

Arachnidæa: Line Drawings

I.

Extravagance at dawn—
your finest threads are strung with pearls
and you, a brooch with a clasp.
Magnify the shiny spheres
to divine that each conceals
a miniature, an image
of struggling wings, of life undone.
Pass at the critical angle
and they flash and snap in the sun.

II.

These haunts are hung haphazardly
with votive offerings, each sucked dry;
paper maché sarcophagi,
cruel chrysalis for moth or butterfly.

III.

Serial killer.
Insecticide, the skill
in which you specialize.

Can we call it murder if nerves connect
not to brain but to canister, chain and gear,
if the dumb drive to survive directs
your every move? Or is it fear
that fuels your addiction to others' pain,
a numbness spreading through the vein
as you rehearse, again, this ritual play—
bind and consume in your quick, kinetic way.

IV.

A stickler for particulars,
you're helpless to repel
the pull of perpendicular
the lure of parallel.

Do lines and circles insulate?
Can order keep at bay
the random drafts that propagate
contagion, death, decay?

The cords are taut. You draw control
from patterns meant to thwart
unraveling, but the tension takes its toll
on the mental weft and warp.

V.

A concert in the round!
Divertimenti scored for eight short hands
will be played by the maestro
for adoring fans.

The fine fretwork glistens.
The strings tune and go still.

Once in motion,
you dazzle in the parts for pizzicato,
leap with ease over fourths and fifths,
scuttle up scales to a dizzying height
then plummet, by octaves, to the sublime.
All are amused, for a time.

The circle is crossed by chords,
point to counterpoint,
illusions of balance, of words.

Listen to the last mournful strains
murmuring a requiem for the days.

VI.

The hours molt and fall away;
the year grows late.
Your web's worn watch face ticks in whispers
and you pray that you will hibernate but briefly
and somehow wake.
As if by grace, the breaths of winter
fog the panes,
leave no trace
of love
or joy
or even hate.
There are, in the end,
only the frayed strands of time,
the failing light
and you, splayed at the center,
condemned to wait.

SEEDS

A goldfinch whose yellow rivals the sun
could cull any bloom this garden has grown
yet favored a flowering long past blown,
its petals shriveled, stem brittle and dun
in a coneflower patch where just this one
seemed to wither, wilt and ask to be mown.
The bird plucked the seeds ensconced in the cone,
made it sway the way that metronomes run
till time runs out, till the goldfinch has flown.
One flower spent, the perennials sown—
a fête conceived by the dying and done
(though death, it's said, may breed oblivion).
So many seeds were borne by each alone,
so many lost with loss of those I've known.

Leaves

For Shinayo Matsumoto

At ninety-one,
she still liked to arrange things
just so,
kept her possessions in tidy boxes,
some engraved with Asian motifs—
dragonflies, exotic birds,
and leaves of bamboo.

And how she loved her sumo!
To watch, on the Japanese channel,
rikishi ten times her size
colliding like forces of nature
filled her with a sense of nostalgia
and possibility.

She was the venerable priestess of tea.
In the autumn of her age,
faithful to the rituals
of a dying art,
she distilled from the parched leaves
this pure nectar,
green as youth.

Flowers found perfection
in her hands,
wrinkled hands, with fingers like twigs.
Once, perhaps, as she trimmed the leaves,
she remembered a time when she
was that perfect flower,
blooming in her kimono
of peach and green.

Her family arranged
a simple Buddhist ceremony.
In late November, the trees
were mostly bare.
But across the lawn, beyond
the small gathering
and the somber stones,
the leaves all danced in the air.

Syringe

Syrinx was a chaste water nymph who, pursued by Pan, was mercifully transformed into hollow reeds. By all accounts, she knew nothing of multiple sclerosis.

I.

These marks, my metric
of defiance and decline,
gauge a meniscus as the lumen fills
with fresh platoons of synthetic drug,
game as ever to deploy.
But what draws my eye this time
is the glint of syringe
—that crack in the slats where sun leaks through—
I pry the blinds,
peer in

II.

As if the brain were lit by a strobe, flickering
between real and not, between now
and some taproot of time,
as if the temporal lobe had seized
on this pool in the skin, this fluid lens,
and telescoped instead
                    to a pond near woods
                              with frogs and nymphs and fish,
                                        and by the water's edge
  a stand of reeds—horsetail, I surmise, *cauda equina*—
        piercing the surface like needles

No plunger
drives the sun to its zenith,
retracts the shadows of trees,
pressures the breeze
to be wind,
nor does the mind,
which thinks it sees
the white coats of birches
but is more akin
to that orange disc climbing through branches
synaptic in all the circuitry

Nights,
when ripples are obsidian,
the moon
spills across the surface,
scatters a flotilla of lights
whose oily spangles buoy, conjoin
yet always part

And here, in that timeless dark,
Syrinx appears
a synthesis of moons
sheathed in halos of myelin film,
the flutings whorled
around her waist
like petals,
that place
where now she glides
an arm, the wrist turned in,
and effortlessly loosens the ties
that linens might slip from her skin

III.

This bloating sloughs
like fat off bone.
I return to burned-out husks
the columns collapsed
the cry of syllables
huddled in shelters
each vowel a child dragging its feet.
Where wires are down
a wireless crackles
and static animates the screen
save for this glimpse of a green frog in my fist
and the teacher saying *insert the needle here,*
between the vertebrae,
then wiggle back and forth
to pith the cord

My reeds become water,
my memories
myth

Locomotion

I know these rails of whining steel
are really spines, the ties but ribs,
and marking them, can't help but feel
a permanence in their grids.

What more would I learn, leaning out
for a clearer view of the track and rubble
should the *Evening Express* on the opposite route
pop my skull like a bubble...

Narcissus

We move in sync and, no surprise,
sport matching foreheads, philtra, chins
and wear identical wire-rims
to improve the view from our duplicate eyes.

Divided we balance, and balanced, excite
inertia. I worship that image for hours,
absorb the minutiae, reflect on the power
of habit, rapture, and this litany of light.

But left and right are flipped and skewed
—cracks in the mirror, ripples on the pond—
the lines of sight project beyond
mere vanity and verisimilitude.

A perfect pane, it lies between
this outer and this inner space
and blocks our coming face to face
with who we are and who we seem.

Nasal Biopsy

Nurse says there's a *mass.* I hear
a requiem, see gothic arches where
alae and columella frame a nare
and its twin. *Is it malignant?* Ushering this fear
to my cathedral, I marvel how breath is born of air
at the portals, inspiring the choirs comingling there.
The priest wafts in, hovers in his shimmering chimere,
but as he places the wafer on a tongue of gauze to share
with *Pathology,* I have to wonder: Is it fair
that a god should mete out grace or despair
in proportion to fealty, that the hereafter (if not the here)
should hinge on professions of faith? Does this square
with cycles of nature? And what of those who dare
to breathe in silence, mutes in the kingdom of prayer?

Tube

Crest seemed apt at a time when I
was iconic:
cylindrical chest,
torso tapered to a terminal seam,
gleaming
and clean as an airfoil.

As my only vowel was O
I tended toward reticence,
though when pressed,
a wave would empower the sea-blue gel
till bluish expressions egressed.

I've since done a lot of shrinking.
My affect's flat
while the lack of limbs has left me bereft
of the gestures of affection—
a hermetic seal
on its shelf.

Mornings
find me cupped in a supple hand,
and I dutifully dispense the drib required
though afterward,
I'm even more depressed.

The mirror says
my rear end's collapsed
and my cap looks like a fez.

In equal measure, contents diminish
and the dim, inner dimensions close in,
hence no holes or fissures,
no pockets of air to squeeze—
no cavities.

In the end,
after all the paste is secreted
and drained as waste,
and my tube is a rumpled wreck of tin,
I still persist—
not dead or empty, just

depleted.

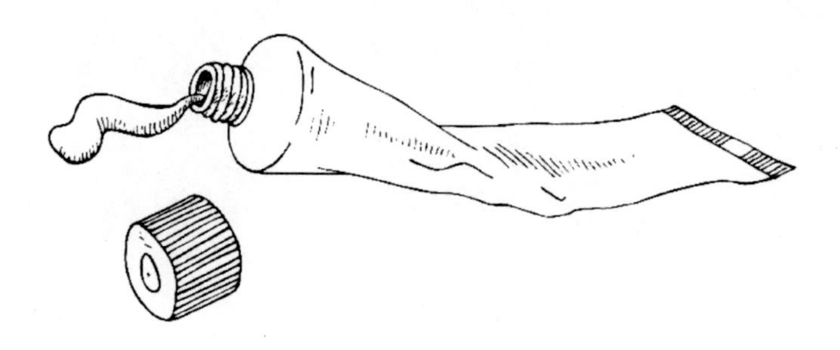

Metamorphosis

The butterfly bush on our berm, *Abelia chinensis,*
grew to resemble some great green sphere
whose blooms and perfume intoxicate the senses
of the black-veined yellow swallowtails. Each year,
they'd congregate on the shrub, reveal to a viewer
how unafraid they are, as when one would pose,
flutter a moment to find a new flower,
then open and fold its wings while nectar flows.
But in May — *Roaches! Panic! Pesticide spray*
for the house, plus perimeter treatment to box in
the yard! Now, the butterflies are gone. They
naturally perished, the caterpillars yellowed with toxin.
It's a shame to be sure, and surely no one's to blame,
though our berm, and world, will never be quite the same.

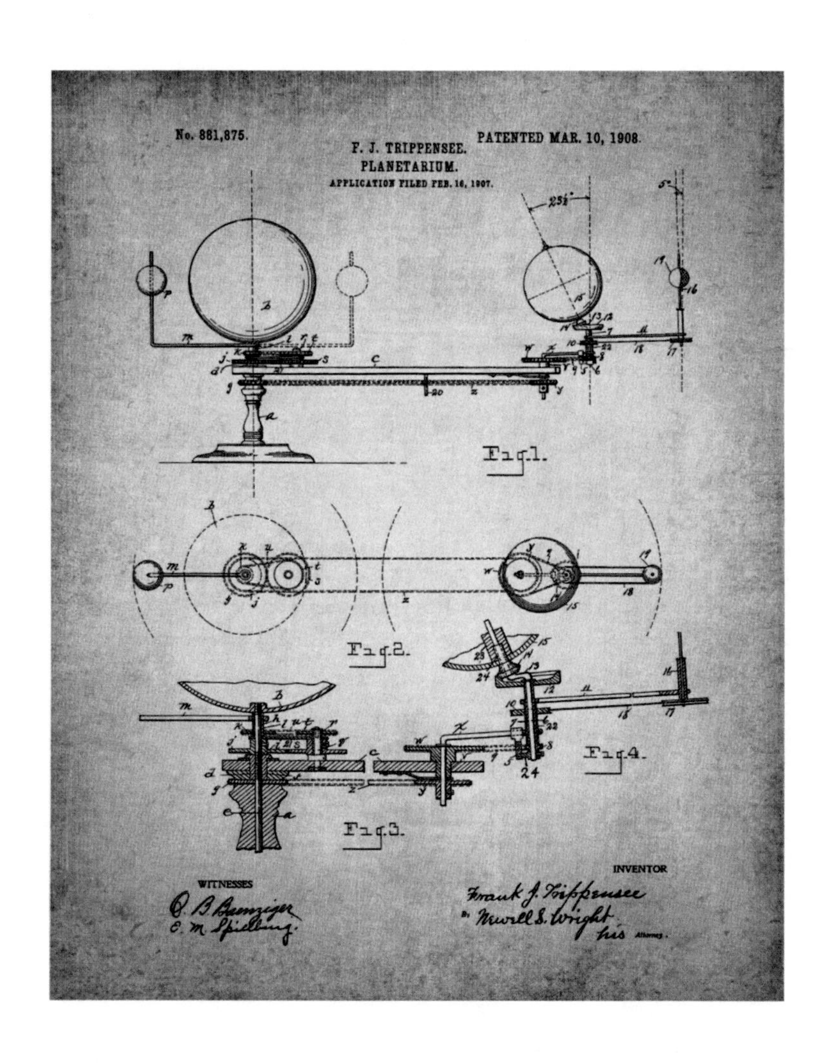
No. 881,875.
F. J. TRIPPENSEE.
PLANETARIUM.
APPLICATION FILED FEB. 16, 1907.
PATENTED MAR. 10, 1908.
Fig.1.
Fig.2.
Fig.3.
Fig.4.
WITNESSES
INVENTOR

(eclipse)

. . . filled Moon with an umber shaft,
obscured the curves the light left bare,
unearthed a cloak to mask
her arch in air

till the tango of spheres resumed, unlinked
our lines, her face, whitened from the
blinding rays, whirling out of sync,
out of umbra and penumbra . . .

ZOMBIE FIRES

North of the boreal forests, the arctic burned,
but since these fires were new to the planet's plight,
one might well have wondered how they earned
their moniker. Experts claimed that lightning might
have kindled combustion—infernos smoldering in
crypts of permafrost for months or years
like beasts feeding on flesh beneath the skin.
Swelter and melts ignited other fears:
cracks breeding in the crust, methane clouds
issuing from fissures, and in the end, a mixture
of ash and soot that blackened the snow like shrouds.
If these repulse, try instead to picture
a ballerina as she pirouettes on pointe,
circles round the star, lifeless in the void.

War Crimes

That spring
when I was five
I burned a hole
in the wing
of a butterfly—
not deceased
but alive
and whole
and wanting to be released.

Neither magnified views
of iridescence
nor the presence
of veins or hues
captured my interest or sight.
Instead, I opted to use
the glass to weaponize rays of light,
holding it exactly one
focal length from a wing meant to beat,
focusing the sun
and ungodly heat.

And because I held the insect tight,
the straining muscles of flight
caused its body to writhe from within,
and despite my hold,
the free wing tried its best to fold
over and shield its tortured twin.

I recall the blister of flame
and the wisp of smoke
swirling up from that child's game
or joke.

I could not have known that day
of bodies burned, of lives lost,
or mused how cruelty and war
were seared in our DNA,
could not have seen what came before—
the camps, the gas, the Holocaust,
Tutsi corpses stacked in piles,
lynchings, like carnivals, greeted with grins,
the killing fields, the Salem trials,
a village bombed, a child's limb.

My parents asserted compliance
with norms, without apology:
He's just too young to fathom pain.
It highlights his love of science.
Born with a brain
for entomology!
In that vein,
the man and woman
who raised me
offered every excuse
one might contrive,
but none of any use.

The horror was human
and the fact that I was five.

Ash

Late in the day she sees
mostly sun behind the trees,
crackling in a maze.

Dusk returns
and silhouettes of branches burn
through embers of a blaze.

Though midnight's indigo fires
enthrall these throngs of naked spires,
their blackness stays.

Spine of Dorian Gray

bulb

my portrait
disfiguring canvas
in its attic of vertebrae

see how the frame
depends on cord

and oils
the oils
ooze out of nerves
as if from collapsing tubes
ocher for ulcer
puce for boil
caput mortuum
for whatever remains

the deepest stratum
fibers writhing in a gesso sea

my erstwhile crimes
those damaged lives
now scars etched with palette knives

archive the carnage
to settle accounts

no doubt the picture's hidden
but wheelchair
diaper
refute the fiction
of perfect beauty
perpetual youth

slashing the canvas is moot

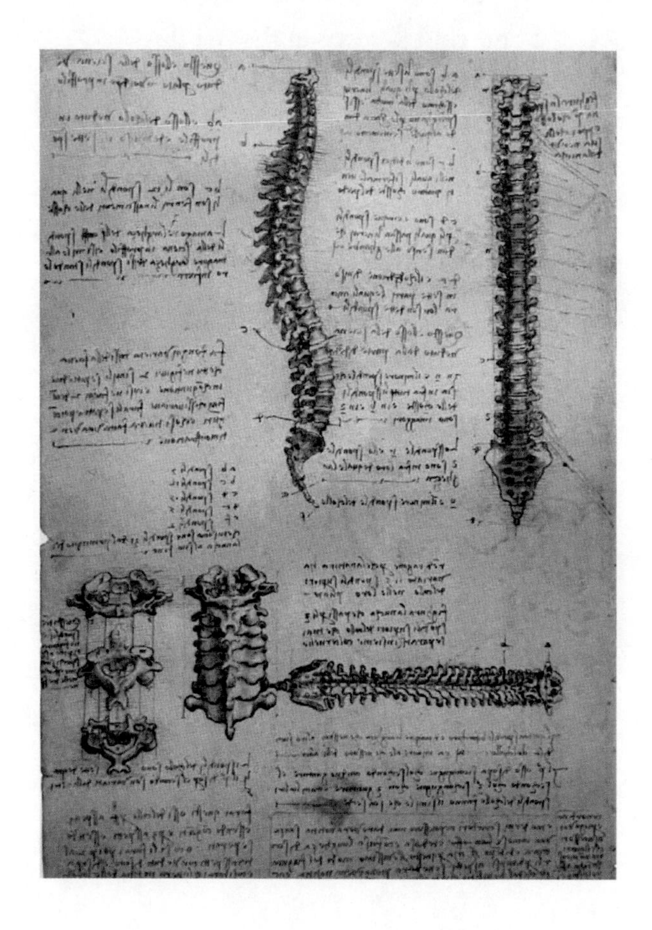

Steve's Balloons

In our dreams,
dreams are like balloons—
light and round and always, always rising.

As I drove through Haw River,
a one-church town in the South,
I caught a glimpse of their maker
and stopped to reflect.

The store was boarded up,
its gravel parking lot weedy
and empty of cars,
and I saw where plastic letters
had been taken down from the faded roof,
leaving a less faded stencil of the words
STEVE'S BALLOONS.

He must have grown up here,
this namesake of mine,
amid these rural ruins,
the porches in disrepair,
the cracked pavement and telephone poles
and the strip mall the locals regard
as their special version of Eden.

I imagined the boyish c
that inflated his hopes
and buoyed his faith
that a worn and weary t
perpetual cause to celebr

I saw then that balloons are not at all round
but are shaped like tears,
that a dream is not so much
that scrap of rubber on the ground
as the breath that once filled it.

Dung Beetles

I.

Nineteen thirty-five, and Escher bores
into a block, sending chips and scrolls
of pearwood flying to the floor, and leaving scores
of tunnels where white will be, plateaus and knolls

for black. The gouge and burin exert the force
he needs for relief, while something else controls
topography, and in darkest ink, restores
two beetles and the ball of dung they roll.

Perhaps the ball is a symbol. A world of waste
that dwarfs the bugs, which grapple nonetheless,
undeterred. And where the pair is placed—
one aft and up, one fore and down—suggest

an artist drawn to natural symmetries,
immersed in black and white, inverted, upright.
The marks become indelible: dichotomies
go spiraling through night and day and night.

II.

Ankh-essen-amun
feeds on her womb.
Swathed in a whitish gauze
sightless,
she is larval
in the stone cocoon.

An amulet exhumes
the shallow cup of her neck—
a scarab
set in green and gold,
its form and folded wings
of serpentine.

Decipher the inscription
(which the carver's lips still whisper):

Great Khepri, source of creation,
as you shall summon the sun from the depths
and wheel the blazing disk across the sky,
so too the beetle moves his ball across the sand,
descends, and creates himself anew.
Go with my queen, oh god of light,
that she may reach the afterworld,
sip life eternal, and renew.

By a winding river, women wail
and men flail their own flesh.

She is dead to all of this.

And so remains
till membranes give,
water comes
and linen bonds dissolve
in a rush of wings.

III.

The frame shifts. Angled glass refracts
the slant of motive and motif, splays the two apart.
As to the endless reflections, know this fact:
What's done is done in mirror, bowel
and art.

Waning Crescent

I see the usual moon. But my daughter contends,
at age four, that the curved sliver of white
is like her new glasses, focusing light
and sharpening the world with only a slender lens.
"Now it's the end of a fingernail!" she pretends,
which prompts me to scan this deepening night
for the long finger, pointing down from a height
toward circumstance no child comprehends.
I'm sure there are sound reasons her sight is clear
and light and resolved for objects stationed far
away from her, yet blind to things so near,
though one can only wonder what they are.
I see... a scythe, and cultivate the fear
its sweeping arc will level every star.

Oak

She conceived
of death as separation, revived
the trope of family trees
whose branches splinter
in the cold, shed
what the ground receives.

So many trees
release their dead
at first freeze,
but the oak, through winter,
holds tight to its leaves.

Cyclone Batsirai, Madagascar, 2022

From the fiery face of a separate sun
and golden shingles upon the sea
comes a reconciliation of shadow and light
softening the fabric of integrity.

Orange disc,
a shimmering film
half-dissolved at its rim
in lucent layers of azure haze,
quivers imperceptibly like a pupil
set on the watery lens of the globe.
Shore overlaps sea like a heavy eyelid
whose lashes are palms in silhouette.
All things imaginable bide in glimpses,
come to naught should the last bead sink
below the horizon, the eye shut itself off
even from darkness. Or is death a blink?

Nights punctuate the transience of light
as though each dark period foreshadows
some longer pause....
whose yawning silence gathers
at the mouth of dusk.
Already, the winds
work the waves into whitecaps,
gusting fine skeins of spray
that twist upward into darkness.
Sheets of rain sweep down increasingly,
beating in dim continuous torrents
that conform to the earth like close wet wings.

Lightning illumines the sea in its throes
the scar of shoreline
and palms, looming like funnels,
their drenched tops blown landward.
Nothing is spared, everything endures,
save when the routed, insatiate winds
swarm to rouse the indecisive sea,
and there howls a squall that meets the land
in a blast of effacing velocity—

∞ ∞ ∞

Though the sky is lined with cloud,
it looks harmless, the color of dried eggshells.
A few gulls litter the beaches,
inspecting the debris for food
or flapping off with a small find.
On the sand, not yet dry, lay stranded
limp filaments of seaweed,
delicate vestiges of boundaries once brimmed
by what has since been utterly transformed.
The storm is over.
In the broad flat estuaries
where uncountable islands
lay down a web of channels
fanning out to sea,
the reeds are flattened,
barely acknowledging the chilly breeze.
At a fork in one of the channels,
cradled among rushes, is a small nest,
carefully woven out of brown fibers.
Inside is a cluster of broken eggshells,
the infant young
nowhere to be found.

Flower Myth

Three years, and we've lost our taste for covid—
the counts the cures the clashes, what love did
to make a plague of grief. Better that Ovid
pen his flower myth: this meadow clovered
and blossoming, this field of rest, the sky above it.

Acknowledgments

"Arachnidæa: Line Drawings" was awarded 2nd prize for the 2020 OPA Poet's Choice Award and was published in Volume 25 of *Verseweavers*.

"Leaves" was published in the Spring 2020 issue of *Buddhist Poetry Review.*

"Syringe" was shortlisted for the 2018 Live Canon International Poetry Competition and was published in *Live Canon Anthology 2018*.

"Locomotion," "Ash" and "Spine of Dorian Gray" were published in Volume 3, Issue 3 of *Coffin Bell,* 2020.

"Narcissus" was a finalist for the 2019 Morton Marr Poetry Prize.

"Nasal Biopsy" was published in Volume 56 of *Pinesong*.

"Zombie Fires" and "Oak" received honorable mentions in the 91st Annual Writer's Digest Competition.

"Steve's Balloons" was awarded 2nd prize for the 2020 Thomas H. McDill Award and was published in Volume 56 of *Pinesong.*

"Waning Crescent" was published in the Fall 2020 issue of *The Road Not Taken.*

Artwork Index